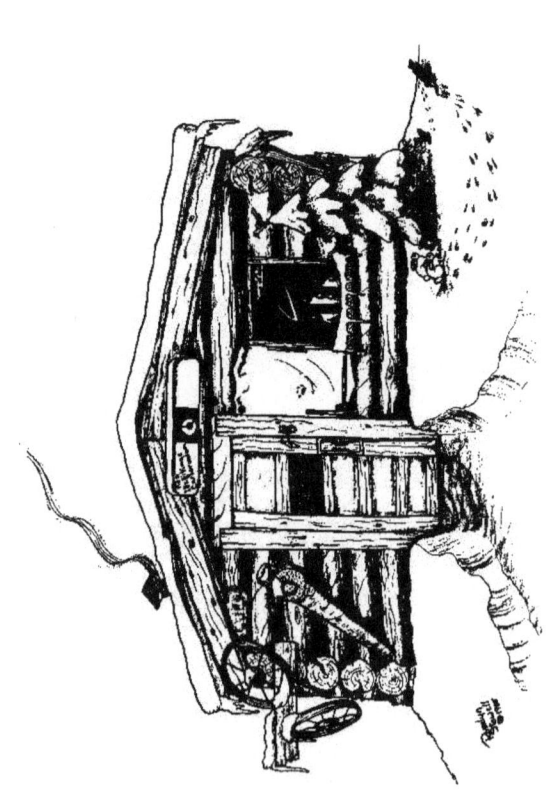

All Rights reserved. Except for use in any review, the reproduction or utilization of this work in whole or in part in any form by any electronic, mechanical or other means, now known or hereafter invented, including xerography, photocopying and recording, or in any information storage or retrieval system, is forbidden without the written permission of the author or her heirs.

Copyright 2014
Publisher: R. E. Stowell
Fairbanks, Alaska

THE RECIPES IN THIS BOOK UTILIZE THE MOST ABUNDANT PROTEIN SOURCE IN ALASKA. HOWEVER, DUE TO PREJUDICE OR WHATEVER, MOST PEOPLE REFRAIN FROM INDULGING.

THESE RECIPES ARE **NOT** INTENDED FOR HUMAN CONSUMPTION, ALTHOUGH WITH A FEW MINOR CHANGES.......

ENJOY

CHECK THE GAME LAWS FOR YOUR AREA BEFORE USING SOME OF THE ANIMALS LISTED AS INGREDIENTS.

COOKING TERMS

BLANCH – WHAT MOST PEOPLE DO WHEN CONFRONTED WITH THE RECIPES IN THIS BOOK.

DOUGH – IF YOU ARE COOKING THESE RECIPES, YOU PROBABLY DON'T HAVE ANY.

DREDGE – METHOD OF GATHERING EGGS AND LARVAE. 2 1/2 INCH IS SUFFICIENT.

BEAT & BATTER – WHAT GUESTS WILL DO TO YOU IF YOU SERVE THESE DISHES.

WINE – IT MIGHT MAKE THEM QUIT BEATING AND BATTERING YOU.

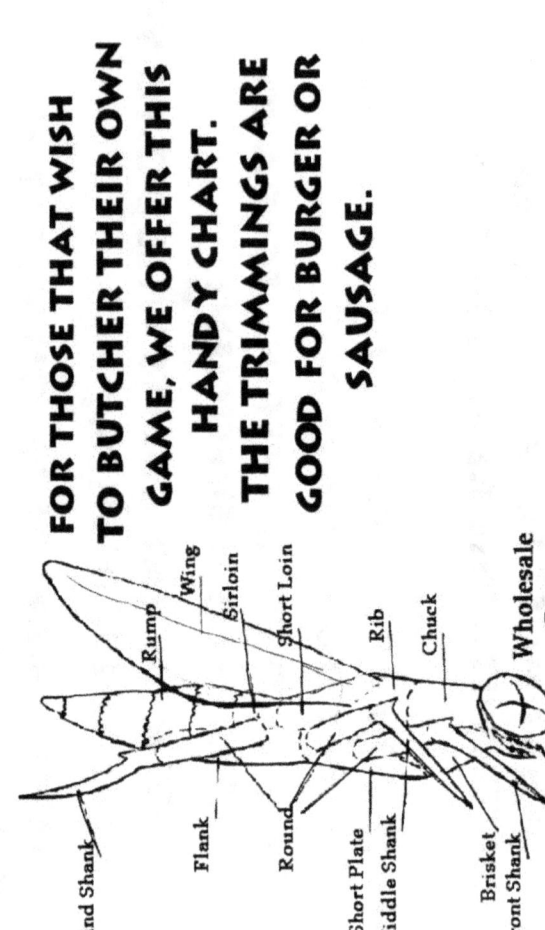

HOW TO CLEAN A MOSQUITO

A SHOWER OR BATH IS QUITE SUFFICIENT.

POLYNESIAN MEATBALLS

MIX 1/2 CUP EVAPORATED MILK, 1/3 CUP MINCED ONIONS, 2/3 CUP CRUSHED SALTINES, 1 TEASPOON SEASON SALT, 1 1/2 POUNDS GROUND SKEETER MEAT. WITH WET HANDS, FORM INTO 1 INCH BALLS. BROWN IN SMALL BATCHES, KEEP WARM. DRAIN 20 OUNCE CAN OF PINEAPPLE TIDBITS, SET TIDBITS ASIDE. TO JUICE ADD 2 TABLESPOON CORNSTARCH, 1/2 CUP CIDER VINEGAR, 2 TABLESPOONS SOY SAUCE, 2 TABLESPOONS LEMON JUICE, 1/2 CUP BROWN SUGAR. COOK IN SKILLET USED TO BROWN MEATBALLS. BRING TO A BOIL, STIRRING CONSTANTLY, UNTIL THICK. ADD MEATBALLS, REDUCE HEAT, COVER & SIMMER 15 MINUTE ADD PINEAPPLE, STIR THROUGH.

SERVE WITH RICE.

TACOS

BROWN CRUMBLED MOSQUITO CHORIZO IN HOT SKILLET. FILL HOT CORN TORTILLAS HALF FULL, ADD CHOPPED TOMATOES, ONIONS, SHREDDED LETTUCE & CHEESE. ADD SOUR CREAM AND SALSA TO TASTE.

QUICHE

350 DEGREES, 40-45 MINUTES

MIX 1 CUP SHREDDED CHEESE, 1 CUP DICED SKEETERS, 10 OZ FROZEN SPINACH - THAWED - SQUEEZED DRY, 1/4 CUP MINCED ONION, 2 BEATEN EGGS, 3/4 CUP MILK, 3/4 CUP MAYONNAISE (NOT LOW OR NO FAT) TOGETHER AND POUR INTO AN UNBAKED PIE SHELL. BAKE.

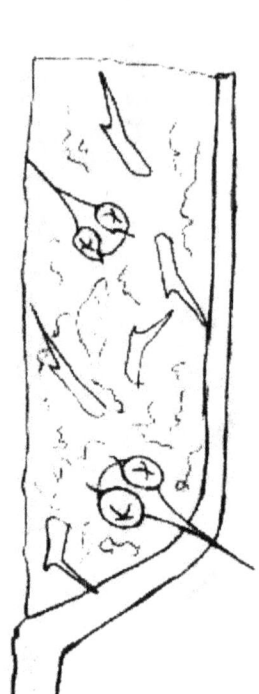

MOSQUITO DEEP-FRIED WINGS

BATTER:
1/2 CUP CORNSTARCH

1/2 CUP FLOUR
3 TBLSPS. SEASON SALT
1 TBLSP. GARLIC SALT
1 12 OUNCE CAN BEER

CUT 2* LARGE WINGS INTO BITE-SIZE PIECES. DIP IN FLOUR, THEN IN BATTER, DEEP-FRY UNTIL BROWNED.

*OR 10,000 SMALL WINGS.

BAKED MOSQUITO

350 DEGREES, 1 HOUR

CLEAN ONE MEDIUM SIZE MOSQUITO. ARRANGE IN A PAN. BASTE OCCASIONALLY WITH PAN JUICES. JUICES WILL RUN CLEAR WHEN DONE. SLICE AND SERVE.

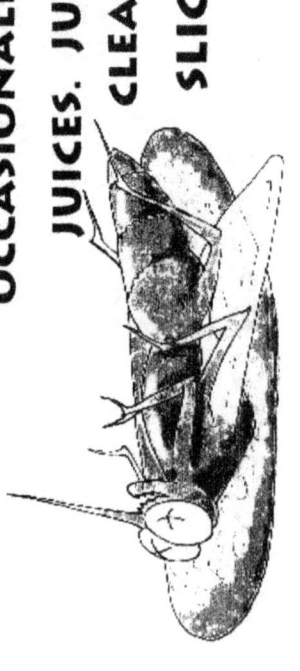

ROAD KILL

DRIVE 100 MILES, SCRAPE WINDSHIELD AND RADIATOR. FORM PATTIES FROM RESIDUE AND GRILL. SERVE ON A BUN WITH ONIONS, TOMATOES AND LETTUCE. CHEESE AND BACON HELP THE FLAVOR. TO HALVE RECIPE, ONLY DRIVE 50 MILES.

HAGGIS

TOAST 5 CUPS DRY OATMEAL, THEN MIX IN 1/2 CUP CHOPPED ONION, 5 TEASPOONS DRY BASIL, 2 TEASPOONS COARSE BLACK PEPPER, 4 TEASPOONS BEEF BOUILLON, 1 1/2 TEASPOONS MACE. KNEAD IN 4 CUPS WATER, 2 1/2 TO 3 POUNDS CHOPPED MEAT (USUALLY INCLUDES OFFAL*) & 1/2 POUND SUET AND 3 EGGS.

PACK INTO CLEANED STOMACH OF ANY LARGE ANIMAL - MOOSE, BEAR, MOSQUITO.....

TIE OPEN ENDS, BOIL FOR 1 TO 1 1/2 HOURS, UNTIL IT FLOATS AND INTERNAL TEMPERATURE REACHES 180 DEGREES.

*OFFAL IS INTERNAL ORGANS, HEART, LIVER, ETC.

SASQUATCH SQUASH

PLACE ZUCCHINI ON TRAIL FREQUENTED BY SASQUATCHES.

WHEN SASQUATCH BENDS DOWN TO PICK UP ZUCCHINI, ROLL BOULDER ONTO HIM. PRESTO — SASQUATCH SQUASH!

SKEETER KABOBS

Make sauce of 1 cup teriyaki sauce, 1/2 cup pineapple juice, 1/2 cup brown sugar, 6 minced garlic cloves, dash of Worcestershire sauce. Marinate 1 pound mosquito chunks in half the sauce for at least 8 hours. On metal or soaked wood skewers, alternate chunks, whole mushrooms, cherry tomatoes, shrimp, strips of green pepper and quarters of onion. Place on hot grill. Cook remaining sauce with 1 1/2 teaspoons cornstarch 'til thick. Baste kabobs with it. Cook about 20 minutes or until done.

SAUTEED MOSQUITOES & MUSHROOMS

2 POUNDS CLEANED MUSHROOMS
2 TABLESPOONS BUTTER

SAUTE OVER HIGH HEAT WITHOUT LID ON PAN. MOSQUITOES WILL SUPPLY THEMSELVES. SEASON TO TASTE.

SUSHI

FLAVOR COOKED STICKY RICE WITH SEASONED RICE VINEGAR TO TASTE. SPREAD IN EVEN LAYER TO SIDES AND ONE END OF SUSHI WRAPPER (SEAWEED) ARRANGE RAW MOSQUITOES, AVOCADO, CUCUMBER STRIP, COOKED EGG AND CARROT STRIP DOWN CENTER OF RICE. ROLL FROM LONG EDGE TOWARD OPEN SEAWEED SIDE. MOISTEN SEAWEED EDGE BEFORE FINISHING ROLL. MOISTURE HOLDS IT TOGETHER, SLICE, ARRANGE DESIGN ON TOP.

FRIED WONTONS

HAVE 1 12 OUNCE PACKAGE WONTON WRAPPERS READY.

STIR FRY 2 C. SHREDDED CABBAGE, 1 C. BEAN SPROUTS, 1/2 C. SHREDDED CARROTS, 1 C. CHOPPED COOKED MOSQUITO, 1/3 C. SLICED GREEN ONION, 1 1/2 TEASPOON SESAME SEEDS, 1/2 TEASPOON MINCED GINGER, 3 MINCED CLOVES GARLIC, 1 1/2 TEASPOON SESAME OIL. PLACE 1 TABLESPOON MIXTURE IN CENTER OF EACH WRAPPER. COMBINE 1 BEATEN EGG WITH 3 TABLESPOONS WATER. MOISTEN EDGES WITH EGG MIXTURE FOLD OPPOSITE CORNERS OVER FILLING, PRESS TO SEAL. HEAT 3 TABLESPOONS OIL IN LARGE SKILLET, FRY 1 - 2 MINUTES EACH SIDE.

PARMESAN MOSQUITOES

400 DEGREES, 50 - 55 MINUTES

IN LARGE ZIP BAG COMBINE 1 C. FLOUR, 4 TEASPOONS SEASON SALT, 1 TEASPOON GARLIC POWDER, SHAKE 4 POUNDS MOSQUITOES TO COAT. DIP IN A BOWL CONTAINING 2 BEATEN EGGS & 3 TABLESPOONS MILK ROLL IN 1/3 C. GRATED PARMESAN CHEESE & 2/3 C. DRY BREADCRUMBS. PLACE ON WELL-GREASED 15 X 10 INCH PAN. BAKE UNTIL JUICES ARE CLEAR.

SKEETER LOAF
350 DEGREES, 1 HOUR

COMBINE 1/2 CUP KETCHUP, 1/2 CUP QUICK-COOKING OATS 1/4 CUP CHOPPED GREEN PEPPER, 1 EGG, 1 TBLSP. CHOPPED PARSLEY, 1 TBLSP. WORCESTERSHIRE SAUCE, 3 MINCED CLOVES GARLIC, 1/2 TEASPOON DRY BASIL, 1/2 TEASPOON PEPPER, 2 POUNDS CHOPPED MOSQUITOES. SHAPE INTO LOAF, TOP WITH ADDITIONAL KETCHUP. ARRANGE ADDITIONAL MOSQUITOES AS GARNISH.

STUFFED MOSQUITO

HOLD ARM STILL, MOSQUITOES ARE SELF-STUFFING.

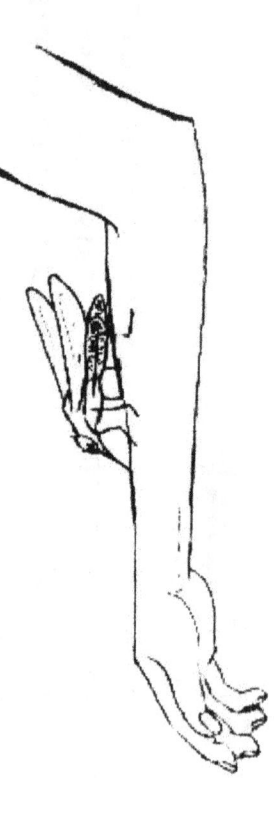

BEAVER FEVER MILK

MIX INSTANT MILK CRYSTALS WITH UNTREATED WATER (FROM ALMOST ANY POND OR STREAM). MIX WELL AND DRINK. WAIT ONE TO FOUR WEEKS FOR SYMPTOMS.

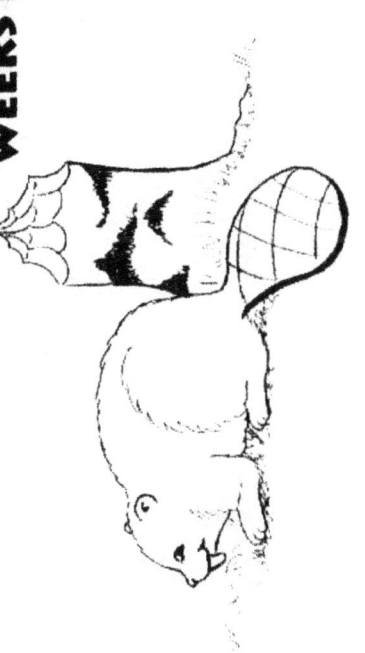

SMOKED MOSQUITO
VERY DIFFICULT TO ROLL, HARD TO LIGHT, ROUGH TO INHALE. HARDLY WORTH THE EFFORT.

MOOSE TRACK SOUP

4 LARGE MOOSE TRACKS, 4 DICED POTATOES,
1 DICED ONION, 2 SLICED STALKS CELERY,
4 SLICED CARROTS, 1 SLICED HEAD OF CABBAGE,
1 CLEANED RABBIT (OPTIONAL, SOME PEOPLE
DO NOT CARE FOR HARE IN THEIR SOUP.)
BOIL UNTIL TENDER, SEASON TO TASTE.

SERVE OVER RICE.

CAVIAR

DREDGE IN A STILL POND WITH A SMALL SUCTION DREDGE. USE SIEVE TO RECOVER EGGS. RINSE EGGS IN LIGHTLY SALTED WATER TO CLEAN. PLACE IN CLEAN SALTY WATER, STRONG ENOUGH TO FLOAT AN EGG FOR 1 - 2 MINUTES. DRAIN WELL, SERVE ON TOAST WITH SOUR CREAM.

THE FOLLOWING 2 RECIPES ARE FROM MY HOW-TO COOKBOOK......

Don't Use A Chainsaw In The Kitchen!!

JELLIED MOOSE NOSE

CUT UPPER JAWBONE OF MOOSE JUST BELOW THE EYES. SKIN AS MUCH AS POSSIBLE, PUT IN LARGE KETTLE OF SCALDING WATER AND PARBOIL 45 MINUTES. REMOVE AND COOL IN COLD WATER. PICK OFF HAIRS LIKE PINFEATHERS FROM A BIRD. WASH THOROUGHLY. PLACE IN FRESH WATER WITH ONION, CRUSHED GARLIC CLOVE, AND 3 OUNCES PICKLING SPICES. BOIL GENTLY UNTIL TENDER, COOL OVERNIGHT IN JUICE. REMOVE BONE AND CARTILAGE. THE BULB OF THE NOSE IS WHITE MEAT, THE THIN STRIPS ALONG THE BONE AND JOWLS ARE DARK MEAT. SLICE OR CHOP THE MEAT THIN AND PACK IN JARS, HEAT THE JUICE TO BOILING AND COVER MEAT, LEAVE 1/2 INCH AIR AT TOP, CLEAN RIMS, PLACE LIDS ON JARS & PROCESS. TO SERVE, CAREFULLY SLIDE OUT OF THE JAR AND SLICE. DO NOT HEAT.

FROM MY HOW-TO COOKBOOK... Don't Use A Chainsaw In The Kitchen!!

BEAVER TAIL

OLD-TIMERS CONSIDER THIS AN EXTREME DELICACY. BLISTER TAIL OVER HOT COALS TILL SKIN LOOSENS OR DIP IN BOILING WATER FOR A COUPLE OF MINUTES. PULL OFF SKIN, LEAVING THE TAIL CLEAN, WHITE AND SOLID. ROAST OR BOIL UNTIL TENDER. MAY BE USED IN PLACE OF PORK WHEN PREPARING BEANS, OR SLICED AND FRIED UNTIL CRISP.

www.ingramcontent.com/pod-product-compliance
Lightning Source LLC
Chambersburg PA
CBHW061349040426
42444CB00011B/3160